I LOVE MUSIC

Rock

Aaron Carr

LET'S READ
AV² BY WEIGL™
ADDED VALUE • AUDIO VISUAL

Go to **www.av2books.com**, and enter this book's unique code.

BOOK CODE

S855489

AV² by Weigl brings you media enhanced books that support active learning.

AV² provides enriched content that supplements and complements this book. Weigl's AV² books strive to create inspired learning and engage young minds in a total learning experience.

Your AV² Media Enhanced books come alive with...

Audio
Listen to sections of the book read aloud.

Video
Watch informative video clips.

Embedded Weblinks
Gain additional information for research.

Try This!
Complete activities and hands-on experiments.

Key Words
Study vocabulary, and complete a matching word activity.

Quizzes
Test your knowledge.

Slide Show
View images and captions, and prepare a presentation.

... and much, much more!

Published by AV² by Weigl
350 5ᵗʰ Avenue, 59ᵗʰ Floor
New York, NY 10118
Website: www.av2books.com

Library of Congress Cataloging-in-Publication Data

Carr, Aaron.
 Rock / Aaron Carr.
   pages cm. -- (I love music)
 Includes bibliographical references and index.
 ISBN 978-1-4896-3593-8 (hard cover : alk. paper) -- ISBN 978-1-4896-3594-5 (soft cover : alk. paper)
 ISBN 978-1-4896-3595-2 (single user ebook) -- ISBN 978-1-4896-3596-9 (multi-user ebook)
 1. Rock music--History and criticism--Juvenile literature. I. Title.
 ML3534.C326 2015
 781.6609--dc23
                        2015003066

Printed in the United States of America in Brainerd, Minnesota
1 2 3 4 5 6 7 8 9 0 19 18 17 16 15

072015
170415

Project Coordinator: Jared Siemens
Designer: Mandy Christiansen

The publisher acknowledges Corbis Images, Getty Images, and iStock as the primary image suppliers for this title.

Rock

CONTENTS

I love music. Rock is my favorite kind of music.

Rock began in the United States in the 1950s.

Rock music came from other kinds of music. It is a mix of American blues and country.

Radio deejays helped rock music become popular.

African Americans made
the first rock songs.

Elvis Presley was one of the first rock stars.

Rock singers often have raw and powerful voices.

Some rock singers can hit very high and very low notes.

Many rock songs are about having fun and falling in love.

Rock songs are often about doing things your own way.

13

The electric guitar is one of the most important instruments in rock.

Les Paul made one of the first electric guitars in 1941.

15

I like to play rock
with my friends.

Playing in a rock band teaches us how to work as a team.

Today, rock bands play shows for large groups of people.

More than 7 million people saw U2 between 2009 and 2011.

I love rock music. Playing music helps me learn new things.

ROCK FACTS

These pages provide detailed information that expands on the interesting facts found in the book. They are intended to be used by adults as a learning support to help young readers round out their knowledge of each musical genre featured in the *I Love Music* series.

Pages 4–5

I love music. Rock is my favorite kind of music. Music is the name given to sounds made with voices or musical instruments and put together in a way that conveys emotion. People use music to express themselves. Rock is one of the most popular forms of music in the world. It is often associated with youth and free expression. Rock music is known for having a strong beat. Other characteristics of rock are hard to define because rock often overlaps other genres.

Pages 6–7

Rock music came from other kinds of music. Rock was born in the mid-1950s, when musicians in the southern United States began mixing rhythm and blues with country to create a new sound. After World War II, many radio stations began playing African American rhythm and blues songs more frequently to fill empty air time. Radio deejay Alan Freed is often credited with naming this kind of music "rock and roll." The popularity of Freed's radio show contributed greatly to rock's popularity.

Pages 8–9

African Americans made the first rock songs. African American rhythm and blues artists such as Chuck Berry were among the first musicians to blend country with rhythm and blues. Arthur "Big Boy" Crudup released what could be considered the first rock song in 1946, with "That's All Right." However, the song did not become popular until Elvis Presley recorded it nearly a decade later. Presley was the first Caucasian singer to popularize the sound African Americans created.

Pages 10–11

Rock singers often have raw and powerful voices. Rock singing focuses more on honest expression than on technique. Many of the best-known rock singers gained fame by being unique. Rock singing can range from lyrical pop-rock styles to the screams or wails often found in hard-rock. With a vocal range of 6 octaves, Mike Patton of rock group Faith No More has one of the widest vocal ranges in rock music today.

Many rock songs are about having fun and falling in love. The wide range of rock music styles has led to an even wider range of lyrical themes. Although songs about love and being yourself have remained common throughout rock history, rock lyrics can be about almost anything. The dominant theme of rock is rebellion, as each generation tries to stand out from those that came before.

The electric guitar is one of the most important instruments in rock. The electric guitar is such a prominent instrument in most rock bands that it could be considered the genre's single defining instrument. Most rock bands are made up of one or more guitarists, a bassist, and a drummer. One or more of these members may also contribute vocals. However, some rock bands have focused more on other instruments, such as pianos or synthesizers.

I like to play rock music with my friends. Playing music with others helps teach children cooperation, teamwork, and how to achieve goals. Children who regularly play music tend to have more confidence and get along better with others. Some students learn better in groups because they do not feel the pressure of having to learn on their own.

Today, rock bands play shows for large groups of people. Rock music is rooted in live performances. Unsigned bands may play small shows at pubs or schools, while established groups signed to a label typically play at large venues. Between 2009 and 2011, Irish rockers U2 grossed more than $730 million on their U2 360° Tour, making it the highest-grossing rock tour to date. More than 7 million people attended one of the tour's 110 worldwide dates.

I love rock music. Playing music helps me learn new things. Recent studies suggest that learning and practicing music can be beneficial to a child's ability to learn. Among these benefits are improved motor skills and dexterity, increased test scores, and even raised Intelligence Quotient, or IQ, scores. Learning music at an early age has also been shown to aid in language development and to improve reading and listening skills.

23

KEY WORDS

Research has shown that as much as 65 percent of all written material published in English is made up of 300 words. These 300 words cannot be taught using pictures or learned by sounding them out. They must be recognized by sight. This book contains 57 common sight words to help young readers improve their reading fluency and comprehension. This book also teaches young readers several important content words. These words are paired with pictures to aid in learning and improve understanding.

Page	Sight Words First Appearance
4	I, is, kind, my, of
5	began, in, states, the
6	a, American, and, came, from, it, other
8	first, made, songs
9	one, was
10	have, often
11	can, high, some, very
12	about, are, many
13	own, things, way, your
14	important, most
16	like, play, to, with
17	as, how, us, work
18	for, groups, large, people, shows
19	between, more, saw, than
20	helps, learn, me, new

Page	Content Words First Appearance
4	music, rock
5	United States
6	blues, country, mix
7	deejays
8	African Americans
9	Elvis Presley, rock stars
10	singers, voices
11	notes
12	fun, love
14	electric guitar, instruments
15	Les Paul
16	friends
17	rock band, team
19	U2

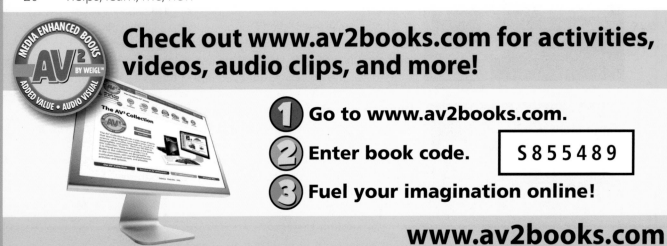

Check out www.av2books.com for activities, videos, audio clips, and more!

1 Go to www.av2books.com.

2 Enter book code. `S 8 5 5 4 8 9`

3 Fuel your imagination online!

www.av2books.com